W9-CBC-397

XTREME RACES
AMERICA'S CUP

BY S.L. HAMILTON

Visit us at
www.abdopublishing.com

Published by ABDO Publishing Company, PO Box 398166, Minneapolis, MN 55439.
Copyright ©2013 by Abdo Consulting Group, Inc. International copyrights reserved in all countries. No part of this book may be reproduced in any form without written permission from the publisher. A&D Xtreme™ is a trademark and logo of ABDO Publishing Company.

Printed in the United States of America, North Mankato, Minnesota.
112012
012013

Editor: John Hamilton
Graphic Design: Sue Hamilton
Cover Design: John Hamilton
Cover Photo: AP (large image) & Getty (small images)
Interior Photos: America's Cup Event Authority-pg 13 (insert), AP/America's Cup Event Authority/Gilles Martin-Raget-pgs 8-9, 12-13, & 23; AP-pgs 1, 10-11, 21 (middle, bottom middle, bottom right) & 27; Corbis-pgs 14-15, 22 (bottom middle), 23 (top), 24-26; Getty Images-pgs 4-5, 16-19, 20 (bottom left & right); 21 (top right), 22 (bottom right) & 28-29; Goodyear-pg 25 (insert); Granger Collection-pgs 6-7 & 20 (top); iStockphoto-pgs 30-32; Library of Congress-pg 22 (bottom left); Thinkstock-pgs 2-3.

ABDO Booklinks
Web sites about Xtreme Races are featured on our Book Links pages. These links are routinely monitored and updated to provide the most current information available.
Web site: www.abdopublishing.com

Cataloging-in-Publication Data

Hamilton, Sue L., 1959-
America's Cup / S.L. Hamilton.
  p. cm. -- (Xtreme races)
Includes index.
ISBN 978-1-61783-692-3
1. America's Cup--History--Juvenile literature. 2. Yacht racing--History--Juvenile literature.
I. Title.
797.1--dc23

2012945702

TABLE OF CONTENTS

America's Cup 4

History 6

Challenger Series 8

The Start 10

The Course 12

The Rules 14

Strategy to Win 16

Dangers 18

Famous Skippers 20

Famous Boats 22

Traditions 24

The Trophy 26

The Finish 28

Glossary 30

Index 32

AMERICA'S CUP

The America's Cup is an international sailing race. It is named after the trophy awarded to the winner. Top sailors and boat designers have competed for the America's Cup for more than 150 years.

Swiss champion Alinghi races against the American challenger BMW Oracle Racing during the 33rd America's Cup in Valencia, Spain, in February 2010.

HISTORY

In 1851, American shipbuilders wanted to prove the speed and quality of their ships. The newly built schooner *America* sailed to England. On August 22, 1851, *America* competed in the Royal Yacht Squadron's 53-mile (85-km) race. *America* won 18 minutes ahead of 14 other ships.

The Royal Yacht Squadron's "One Hundred Guinea Cup" was renamed after the Americans' winning schooner. This "America's Cup" trophy went to the New York Yacht Club. They decided to use the trophy to promote friendly sailing races among nations. The America's Cup was born.

XTREME FACT – *The America's Cup trophy stayed with the New York Yacht Club from 1851 to 1983. In 1983 Australia's Royal Perth Yacht Club won the trophy.*

CHALLENGER SERIES

For 119 years, there was never more than one team at a time that challenged the current America's Cup winner. Since 1970, multiple teams have challenged the winner. A series of races are held between the challengers.

XTREME FACT – *After more than 130 years of racing, only four countries have won the America's Cup: the United States, Australia, New Zealand, and Switzerland.*

These races are called the America's Cup Challenger Series. Races are held in different locations around the world. The winner then races the current America's Cup champion. The final America's Cup race is held in the defender's home waters.

America's Cup competitors sail off Newport, Rhode Island, in June 2012.

The Start

The current America's Cup begins with a "high speed" start. Racers see a large clock counting down. The boats must be in a marked starting area or they are given a time penalty. Racers who cross the starting line too soon are penalized. It takes a lot of skill to time the takeoff just right.

NEW ZEALAND

THE COURSE

The America's Cup race begins at the starting zone. Yachts cross the starting line and build up speed. Buoys or anchored boats are placed in the water to mark the course. The racers must sail around these markers. After a number of laps, the boats head for the finish line.

America's Cup racers practice on a course off Newport, Rhode Island in 2012.

The 2013 America's Cup course in San Francisco Bay is planned so that fans can see the two boats race nearly side-by-side. On race day, the course may be altered depending on the wind strength and direction. The average length of the course is 2.3 miles (3.7 km).

 XTREME FACT – In 2013, the race course in California's San Francisco Bay will bring the boats within 100 yards (91 m) of the shore.

THE RULES

Today's racers compete in catamarans. These boats are fast and nimble, but capsize more easily. The 34th America's Cup rules allow for a crew of 11 during the final races. Crew members must keep their boat inside course boundaries.

Team Korea receives a penalty after crossing the bow of Luna Rossa Swordfish in California's San Francisco Bay in 2010.

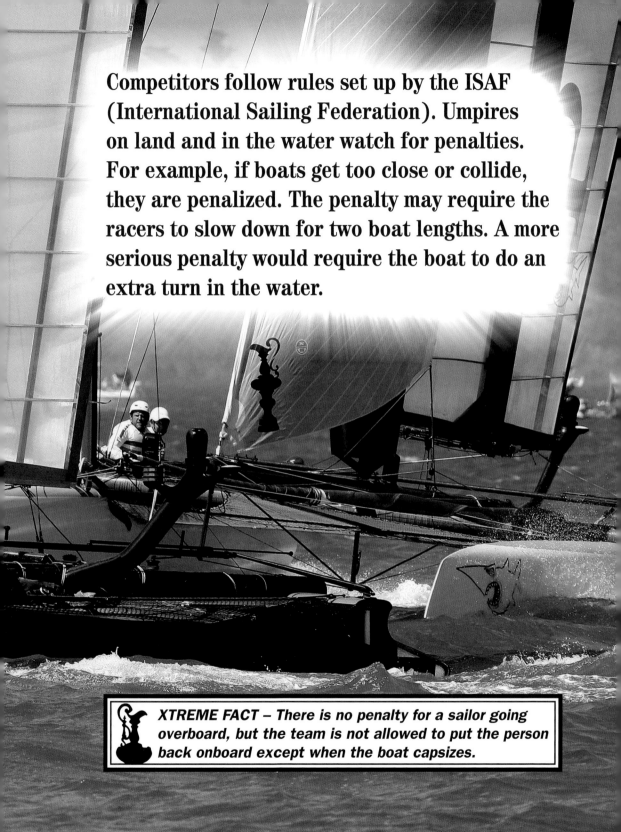

Competitors follow rules set up by the ISAF (International Sailing Federation). Umpires on land and in the water watch for penalties. For example, if boats get too close or collide, they are penalized. The penalty may require the racers to slow down for two boat lengths. A more serious penalty would require the boat to do an extra turn in the water.

XTREME FACT – There is no penalty for a sailor going overboard, but the team is not allowed to put the person back onboard except when the boat capsizes.

STRATEGY TO WIN

Crew members must be strong and athletic. Skippers need to think quickly because the boats are moving at such high speed.

Boats must stay on course and avoid bridges, islands, and the shoreline. Teams must be quick and limit their mistakes to win.

DANGERS

America's Cup boats are big and fast. They race along a tight course. The possibility of a collision is great. Strong winds, currents, and waves are constant threats. One of the greatest dangers is flipping the boat over. Sailers end up in cold water, bruised and battered.

Oracle Team USA tries to hang on after flipping their catamaran while training in San Francisco Bay in October 2012.

FAMOUS SKIPPERS

Winning the America's Cup takes great sailing skill. A few skippers have become famous. They brought out the best in their sailing team and their boats.

John Cox Stevens and eight friends started the New York Yacht Club (NYYC) in 1844. Stevens was named commodore, or president. Their goal was to race sailing yachts. Stevens went on to captain the America, winning the first America's Cup in 1851.

Skippers Dennis Conner (USA) and Russell Coutts (New Zealand) are four-time winners of the America's Cup competitions.

Dennis Conner won the America's Cup in 1974 (as a helmsman), 1980, 1987, and 1988.

Russell Coutts won the America's Cup in 1995, 2000, 2003, and 2010 (as Team CEO).

Charles Barr and Harold Vanderbilt are three-time winners of the America's Cup competitions. Both sailed for the NYYC.

Charles Barr won the America's Cup for the USA in 1899, 1901, and 1903.

Harold S. Vanderbilt won the America's Cup for the USA in 1930, 1934, and 1937.

John Bertrand of Australia's Royal Perth Yacht Club was the first skipper to take the America's Cup away from the United States. In 1983, Bertrand's team, aboard the Australia II, defeated the New York Yacht Club's ship Liberty.

Only three women have competed in a final America's Cup race. All three had the job of timekeeper onboard the yachts.

Hope Goddard Iselin was part of the 1895, 1899, & 1903 teams.

Phyllis Brodie Gordon Sopwith raced in 1934 and in 1937.

Gertrude Conaway Vanderbilt raced in 1934 and 1937.

FAMOUS BOATS

A few America's Cup boats are remembered for their speed, quality, and victories.

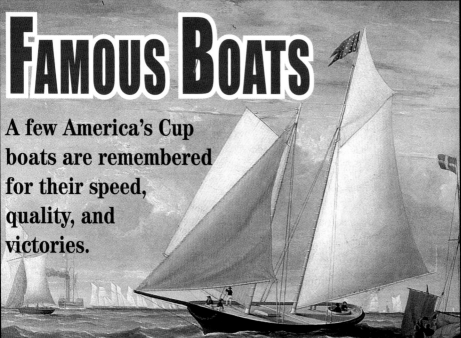

In 1851, America *became the first winner. The ship gave the race and trophy its name.*

The Columbia, Intrepid, *and* Courageous *are the only three yachts to have won the America's Cup twice.*

Columbia *(NYYC-USA) won in 1899 and 1901. The ship was skippered by Charles Barr during both wins.*

Intrepid *(NYYC-USA) won in 1967 and 1970. The ship was skippered by Emil Mosbacher in 1967 and Bill Ficker in 1970.*

Courageous *(NYYC-USA) won in 1974 and 1977. The ship was skippered by Ted Hood in 1974 and Ted Turner in 1977.*

USA's
Liberty

Australia's
Australia II

In 1983, the *Royal Perth Yacht Club's* Australia II *competed against the New York Yacht Club's* Liberty. **Skippered by John Bertrand, the Australia II won, becoming the first yacht in 132 years to take away the America's Cup trophy from the NYYC.**

The 2013 America's Cup competition is being raced with catamarans. The AC45 wing-sailed catamaran will be used for a preliminary series. The final America's Cup will be raced in the AC72, which may make the 34th America's Cup the fastest race yet.

XTREME FACT – *Yachts used in previous America's Cup races had a top speed of 14 knots (16 mph/26 kph). The 2013 boats will race close to 35 knots (40 mph/65 kph).*

TRADITIONS

The first America's Cup race was viewed by England's Queen Victoria in 1851. When the yacht *America* took the lead, the queen asked who was in second place. She was told, "Your Majesty, there is no second." This statement continues to represent the idea that in the America's Cup, only the best wins.

America's Cup races traditionally start and end with the firing of guns. Crews "answer the guns" and start the race.

Beginning in 1928, Goodyear blimps were named after winning America's Cup boats. Goodyear's president thought the blimps were like "yachts in the sky."

The Goodyear blimp Columbia *in 1978.*

THE TROPHY

The America's Cup (opposite page) is the oldest active trophy in international sporting events. The first winner, John Cox Stevens, considered melting the cup to make medallions for each of his sailors. It was decided instead that the trophy should be a "Deed of Gift." The trophy is kept by the winning club until a new winner claims it.

Since 1983, the Louis Vuitton Cup is awarded to the winner of the America's Cup Challenger Series. Racing teams from around the world compete to become the "Challenger of Record" against the standing America's Cup winner. Four out of the seven winners of the Louis Vuitton Cup have gone on to win the America's Cup.

From 1851 to 2010, only six yacht clubs have won the sterling silver America's Cup trophy: New York Yacht Club, Royal Perth Yacht Club, San Diego Yacht Club, Royal New Zealand Yacht Squadron, Société Nautique de Genève, and the Golden Gate Yacht Club.

 XTREME FACT – In 1997, the America's Cup was smashed by a protester in New Zealand. It was restored by London's Garrard, the company that created it in 1848.

THE FINISH

The final America's Cup is a series of match races. The two best yachts and crews face off against each other. Only one team will conquer the wild winds and waters to become America's Cup winners.

Switzerland's Team Alinghi beats New Zealand's Emirates Team in the close 2007 America's Cup race.

GLOSSARY

BUOY
An anchored floating marker. Buoys are used to warn sailors of hazards in the water. In the America's Cup races, buoys are used to mark the course.

CAPSIZE
To turn over. Wind and waves may cause a boat to capsize in the water.

CATAMARAN
A sailboat with two hulls or floats connected by a deck or a frame. Lightweight, fast, and maneuverable, catamarans are the chosen boat for the 34th America's Cup races.

INTERNATIONAL SAILING FEDERATION (ISAF)
The group that develops the rules for the sport of competitive sailing. America's Cup racers follow the ISAF rules.

Knot

In racing, a unit of speed equaling one nautical mile per hour. One nautical mile per hour is equal to 1.151 miles per hour or 1.852 kilometers per hour.

Match Race

A race where two identical boats compete against each other. Match races usually take about 20 minutes.

Schooner

A large sailing ship with at least two masts.

Skipper

The person who commands a ship. Also called the captain.

Timekeeper

A crew member's position on an America's Cup team in the early- to mid-1900s. The timekeeper decided when to turn for the starting line at a time when giant yachts (123-143 feet/37-44 m long) were not as nimble as modern racing boats. The timing for this was very important to win the race.

Yacht

A sailing boat or powered boat used for pleasure. Not a working boat.

INDEX

A

AC45 catamaran 23
AC72 catamaran 23
Alinghi 4, 29
America (schooner) 6, 20, 22, 24
America's Cup (trophy) 7, 21, 23, 26, 27
America's Cup Challenger Series 9, 26
Australia 7, 8, 21
Australia II 21, 23

B

Barr, Charles 21, 22
Bertrand, John 21, 23
BMW Oracle 4

C

California 13, 14
catamaran 14, 23
Challenger of Record 26
Columbia (blimp) 25
Columbia (yacht) 22
Conner, Dennis 20
Courageous 22
Coutts, Russell 20

D

Deed of Gift 26

E

Emirates Team 29
England 6, 24

F

Ficker, Bill 22

G

Garrard (company) 27
Golden Gate Yacht Club 27
Goodyear 25

H

Hood, Ted 22

I

International Sailing Federation (ISAF) 15
Intrepid 22
Iselin, Hope Goddard 21

L

Liberty 21, 23
London 27
Louis Vuitton Cup 26
Luna Rossa Swordfish 14

M

Mosbacher, Emil 22

N

New York Yacht Club (NYYC) 7, 20, 21, 22, 23, 27
New Zealand 8, 20, 27, 29
Newport, RI 9, 12

O

One Hundred Guinea Cup 7
Oracle Team USA 19

R

Rhode Island 9, 12
Royal New Zealand Yacht Squadron 27
Royal Perth Yacht Club 7, 21, 23, 27
Royal Yacht Squadron 6, 7

S

San Diego Yacht Club 27
San Francisco Bay 13, 14, 19
Société Nautique de Genève 27
Sopwith, Phyllis Brodie Gordon 21
Spain 4
Stevens, John Cox 20, 26
Switzerland 8, 29

T

Team Alinghi 29
Team Korea 14
Turner, Ted 22

U

United States 8, 20, 21, 22

V

Valencia 4
Vanderbilt, Gertrude Conaway 21
Vanderbilt, Harold 21
Victoria, Queen 24